Little Baker Kids Cookbook

Fun Baking Recipes for Kids of All Ages

Table of Contents

Introduction 4

    Recipe 1. Monkey Tray Bake 6

    Recipe 2. Chocolate Muddle Cake 8

    Recipe 3. Super-seed Slice 11

    Recipe 4. Chocolate Pizza 13

    Recipe 5. Garlic Dough Balls 16

    Recipe 6. Cheese, Egg and Ham Bakes 18

    Recipe 7. Lemon and Poppy Seed Fête Cake 20

    Recipe 8. Jammy Flying Saucers 22

    Recipe 9. Rock Cakes 24

    Recipe 10. Blueberry Bars 26

    Recipe 11. Apricot and Chia Fingers 29

    Recipe 12. Mini Quiches 31

    Recipe 13. Cheese Straws 33

    Recipe 14. Orange and Lemon Cookies 35

    Recipe 15. Seed and Herb Muffins 37

    Recipe 16. Protein Bakes 39

    Recipe 17. Cheese and Chive Soda Bread Balls 41

Recipe 18. Shortbread 43

Recipe 19. Blondies 45

Recipe 20. Tomato and Mozzarella Puffs 47

Recipe 21. Mini Toads in A Hole 49

Recipe 22. Cherry Flapjacks 51

Recipe 23. Pea and Sweetcorn Pancakes 53

Recipe 24. Pizza Wheels 55

Recipe 25. Death by Chocolate Cookies........................57

Recipe 26. Vanilla and Chocolate Pikelets 60

Recipe 27. Chocolate Hazelnut Kisses 62

Recipe 28. Chocolate Hazelnut Spread (AKA "Nutella") Brownies 65

Recipe 29. Coconut & Raspberry Oaties 67

Recipe 30. Cornflake and Marshmallow Cakes.............69

Introduction

Most kids love to help out in the kitchen, and this often leads to them wanting to make their favorite treats for themselves. The only problem is most cookbooks are written with adults in mind and therefore are long and drawn out. Or worse cluttered with terminology that kids can't understand.

This book on the other hand is written with kids in mind and caters every recipe to them. That means no matter what age you are you'll be able to follow right along. This book will inspire young bakers to better their craft and instill a lifelong love of baking.

Recipe 1. Monkey Tray Bake

Serves: 9

Prep Time: 5 Minutes

Cooking Time: 35 Minutes

The List of Ingredients:

1. Pinch of Salt
2. 3 Eggs
3. 1 tsp Baking Powder

4. 1 cup White Sugar
5. 6oz Chocolate Chips
6. 1 ¾ cups All-Purpose Flour
7. 2 Ripe Bananas (the blacker the better!)
8. 1/4 cup of Milk
9. ¾ cup / 6oz Butter, softened

Method:

Step 1   Preheat the oven to 375°F/190°C/Gas Mark 5 and grease and line a 9" square cake tin.

Step 2   Cream the sugar and butter together until pale and fluffy. Beat in the eggs and milk. Mash the bananas and add to the bowl.

Step 3   Mix the flour, salt, baking powder, and chocolate into the bowl and pour into the prepared tin.

Step 4   Bake for 35 minutes until risen and golden.

Recipe 2. Chocolate Muddle Cake

Serves: 9

Prep Time: 5 minutes

Cooking Time: 35-40 minutes

The List of Ingredients:

1. ½ cup of Butter, softened
2. 1 tsp Baking Powder
3. 1 cup of Buttermilk

4. 2 cups of All-Purpose Flour
5. ¾ cup Cocoa Powder
6. 2 cups of chocolate frosting
7. 2 large Eggs, beaten
8. 2 tsp Baking Soda
9. 1 ¾ cups of White Sugar

Method:

Step 1	Preheat oven to 350°F/180°C/Gas Mark 4 and grease and line an 8" square cake tin.
Step 2	Sift the flour, cocoa powder, and baking agents together and leave to one side.
Step 3	Beat the sugar and butter together until fluffy and light.
Step 4	Gradually beat in the eggs and add a little of the flour if the mix starts to split a little.
Step 5	Add all of the flour and beat very briefly until just combined.
Step 6	Pour into the tin and level. Bake for 35-40 minutes until the cake is risen and cooked.
Step 7	Remove from the oven and cool a little before taking the cake from the tin.

Step 8   Spread the chocolate frosting over the top once the cake has completely cooled and then scatter over the sweets.

Recipe 3. Super-seed Slice

Makes: 9

Preparation Time: 5 Minutes

Cooking Time: 25 Minutes

The List of Ingredients:

1. ¾ cup / 6oz Butter
2. ½ cup of Sunflower Seeds
3. 1/2 cup of Rolled Oats

4. ½ cup of Pumpkin Seeds
5. 4 tbsp Sesame Seeds
6. 1/3 cup of Dark Brown Sugar
7. 1 tbsp Oat brown
8. ¼ cup of Honey

Method:

Step 1   Preheat the oven to 375°F/190°C/Gas Mark 5 and line a 9" square baking tin.

Step 2   Melt the butter, syrup, and sugar together. Add all of the other ingredients and mix well.

Step 3   Press into the baking tray. Bake for 20-25 minutes until crunchy and golden on top.

Recipe 4. Chocolate Pizza

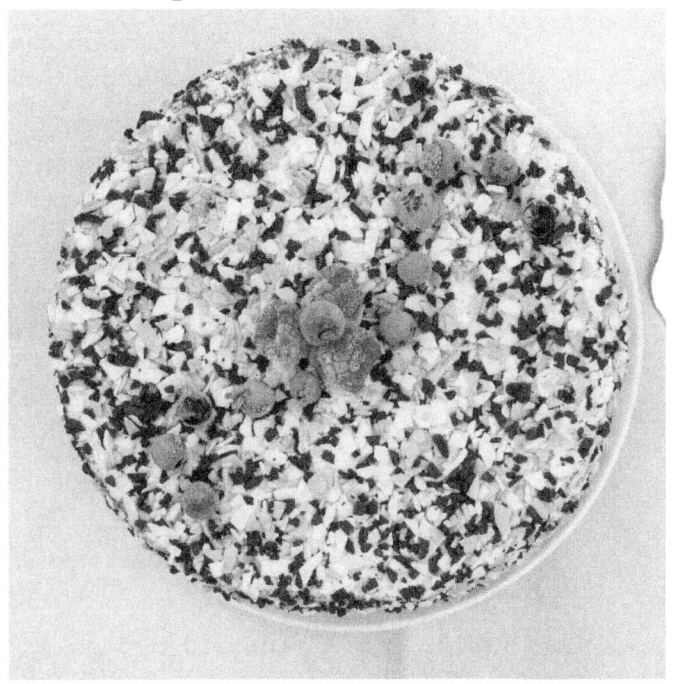

Serves: 10-12

Prep Time: 20 minutes

Cook Time: 20 minutes

The List of Ingredients:

1. A handful of large Colored Marshmallows
2. 1 Egg, beaten
3. ½ cup Light Brown Sugar

4. 1 tsp Vanilla Extract
5. 1 cup of Dark Chocolate
6. 1 cup of M&Ms or other brightly colored chocolate
7. 1 ¾ cups Flour
8. 1 cup of Butter, softened
9. ½ cup Sugar
10. Pinch of Salt
11. ½ cup of Milk Chocolate Chips
12. 1 cup of White Chocolate Chips

Method:

Step 1   Preheat the oven to 375°F/190°C/Gas Mark 5 and line or grease one large baking tray.

Step 2   Mix the flour, sugar, butter, salt, vanilla, and egg together with a wooden spoon to form a stiff dough. Press down onto the baking tray to form one large circle. It should look a little uneven to represent "dough" and should be roughly 1" – 1.5" thickness. Bake in the oven for 25 minutes until golden and crisp.

Step 3   Scatter the marshmallows, white chocolate, and M&Ms over the top. Replace in the oven for 5 minutes to allow the marshmallows to melt and ooze over the crust. Remove from the oven again and allow to cool and harden.

Step 4   When removed from the oven, melt the dark chocolate in a glass bowl over a pan of simmering water.

Step 5   Drizzle the dark chocolate over the top and when hardened, cut into 10-12 wedges.

Recipe 5. Garlic Dough Balls

Makes: 24 Balls Approx.

Preparation Time: 20 minutes

Proving Time: 1 hour

Cooking Time: 15 Minutes

The List of Ingredients:

1. 1 tbsp Garlic Oil
2. 300ml Warm Milk

3. 1 tbsp Dried Yeast
4. 1 tsp Salt
5. 1 tsp Sugar
6. 3 cups of Strong Flour
7. 2 Garlic Cloves, crushed

Method:

Step 1 Preheat the oven to 375°F/190°C/Gas Mark 5 and grease and line a baking tray.

Step 2 Add all of the ingredients together and either knead using a bread hook on a processor or knead on a floured surface by hand. After 8-10 minutes and when the dough is soft and elastic, leave in an oiled bowl, covered, and allow to prove in a warm place for 1 hour.

Step 3 Give the dough a good knead to remove the air and then roll into approximately 24 balls.

Step 4 Place on the baking tray and bake in the oven for 15-20 minutes until risen and cooked.

Recipe 6. Cheese, Egg and Ham Bakes

Serves: 4

Prep Time: 10 minutes

Cooking Time: 10 minutes

The List of Ingredients:

1. 4 tsp Tomato Ketchup
2. 4 Handfuls of Grated Cheese
3. 4 Eggs

4. 4 Slices of Ham
5. 4 Large Flour Tortillas

Method:

Step 1　Preheat the oven to 375°F/190°C/Gas Mark 5 and grease and line a baking tray.

Step 2　Lay the wraps out flat. Place a piece of ham into the center of each. Top with the grated cheese. Make a dent in the grated cheese and carefully crack an egg onto each. Top with the tomato ketchup.

Step 3　Carefully fold each edge of the wrap into the center, to create a square. Slide each wrap onto an individual piece of foil and tightly fold the foil around the wrap, to keep it secure and leakproof.

Step 4　Add to the baking tray and bake for 10 minutes. Careful, the insides will be quite hot!

Recipe 7. Lemon and Poppy Seed Fête Cake

Serves: 8

Prep Time: 5 Minutes

Cooking Time: 45 Minutes

The List of Ingredients:

1. ¾ cup of Milk
2. 1 cup White Sugar

3. 3 tbsp Poppy Seeds
4. 1 tsp Baking Powder
5. ¾ cup / 6oz Butter, softened
6. 3 Eggs
7. 2 Lemons, zest and Juice
8. 1 ¾ cups All-Purpose Flour

Method:

Step 1   Preheat the oven to 350°F/180°C/Gas Mark 4 and grease and line a 1 lb. loaf tin.

Step 2   Cream the sugar and butter together, until fluffy and light. Beat in the milk and eggs. Add the flour, lemon juice, lemon zest, baking powder, and poppy seeds then mix well to combine.

Step 3   Add the mix to the prepared tin and bake for 45 minutes, until risen and cooked through. If you want to pre-slice this, wait until it has cooled completely first.

Recipe 8. Jammy Flying Saucers

Makes: 18 Flying Saucers

Prep Time: 4 minutes

Cooking Time: 25 Minutes

The List of Ingredients:

1. ½ cup of cold Butter, cubed
2. ¼ cup of Jam
3. Pinch of Salt

4. 1 cup of Flour
5. 3 tbsp Sugar

Method:

Step 1   Preheat the oven to 375°F/190°C/Gas Mark 5 and line or grease 2x baking trays.

Step 2   Rub the butter into the flour with your hands, until it becomes fine breadcrumbs. Stir in the sugar.

Step 3   Using a little ice-cold water, mix the dry ingredients together to form a stiff dough.

Step 4   Roll out on a floured surface or board until 1" thick. Cut out 18 round disks using a cookie cutter and place on the baking trays. Using the back of a spoon, press down in the center of each cookie to make a deep indent. Bake for 20-25 minutes until golden and cooked. Cool on a wire rack.

Step 5   When the cookies are cooled, heat the jam a little bit to make it a bit thinner and carefully spoon into the center of each indent. Allow to cool and serve.

Recipe 9. Rock Cakes

Makes: 12

Prep Time: 10 Minutes

Cooking Time: 30 Minutes

The List of Ingredients:

1. ½ cup / 3 ½ oz Butter, unsalted and fridge cold
2. 1 1/2 tsp Baking Soda
3. 1 Egg

4. 2 cups All-Purpose Flour
5. 1 tsp Vanilla Extract
6. 2/3 cup Dried Fruit
7. 2-3 tbsp Milk
8. ½ cup White Sugar

Method:

Step 1 Preheat the oven to 400°F/200°C/Gas Mark 6 and line a large baking tray.

Step 2 Cut butter into small cubes. Add the flour and butter to a bowl and rub the butter cubes using your fingertips in. Keep going until flour looks like breadcrumbs and there are no lumps.

Step 3 Stir in the sugar and dried fruit.

Step 4 Beat the egg with the vanilla and stir into the mix. Add enough milk to form a dry dough, which can still be dropped from a spoon.

Step 5 Drop 12 heaps of the mix onto the baking tray and bake for 25-30 minutes, until cooked and golden.

Recipe 10. Blueberry Bars

Makes: 9

Preparation Time: 15 Minutes

Cooking Time: 30-40 Minutes

The List of Ingredients:

1. 3 tbsp Water
2. ½ cup of White Sugar
3. 4 tsp Cornstarch

4. 2 cups of Rolled Oats
5. 1 cup of Light Brown Sugar
6. 1 tsp Cinnamon
7. ½ tsp Baking Soda
8. 3 cups of Blueberries, fresh or frozen
9. ¾ cup of Butter, softened
10. 3 tbsp Lemon Juice

Method:

Step 1   Preheat the oven to 375°F/190°C/Gas Mark 5 and line a 9" square baking tin.

Step 2   Heat the blueberries, lemon juice, water, and sugar in a saucepan. Heat until it reaches a boil and cook for 10 minutes until the blueberries are syrupy and broken down a little. Stir in the cornstarch and cook for a further few minutes to thicken. Allow to cool completely.

Step 3   In a bowl, mix all the other ingredients. Pat half of the mix into the bottom of the baking tin and press down firmly. Pour the cooled blueberry mixture on top. Finish off by sprinkling over the remaining oat mixture and pressing down a little.

Step 4   Bake for 30-40 minutes until crisp and golden.

Recipe 11. Apricot and Chia Fingers

Makes: 9

Preparation Time: 5 minutes

The List of Ingredients:

1. ½ tsp Cinnamon
2. 5 tbsp Sunflower/Pumpkin Seeds
3. 2/3 cup Rolled Oats
4. 4oz Dark Chocolate, chopped
5. 2 tbsp Honey

6. ½ cup Chopped Dates
7. 2 tbsp Chia Seeds
8. ½ cup Chopped Dried Apricots
9. 2 tbsp Sesame Seeds

Method:

Step 1 Preheat the oven to 375°F/190°C/Gas Mark 5 and line a 9" square baking tin.

Step 2 Place all of the ingredients (apart from the chocolate) in a food processor. Blend until the mix is quite broken down and has become a coarse mix. Stir in the chocolate chunks.

Step 3 Press into the baking tray. Bake for 20-25 minutes until crunchy and golden on top.

Recipe 12. Mini Quiches

Makes: 12

Preparation Time: 10 minutes

Cooking Time: 30 minutes

The List of Ingredients:

1. 1 tsp Salt
2. 8oz Shortcrust Pastry Ball
3. 1 ¼ cups of Milk

4. 3 eggs
5. 1 cup of Grated Cheese
6. 1 cup of Finely Chopped Ham

Method:

Step 1   Preheat the oven to 375°F/190°C/Gas Mark 5 and grease a 12-hole muffin tin.

Step 2   Roll the pastry out and cut circles to fill the muffin holes. Using baking paper and baking beans, fill each hole and place in the oven for 10 minutes to help the pastry crisp up.

Step 3   Meanwhile, whisk the eggs, milk, ham, cheese, and salt together.

Step 4   Remove the pastry from the oven and take off the paper and beans. Carefully pour the mix into each hole and return to the oven for a further 20 minutes, until the filling is set and golden on top.

Recipe 13. Cheese Straws

Makes: 15-16 Approx.

Prep Time: 5 minutes

Cooking Time: 20 Minutes

The List of Ingredients:

1. 1 cup of Grated Cheese
2. 1 Large Sheet of Puff Pastry
3. 1 Egg, beaten

Method:

Step 1   Preheat the oven to 400°F/200°C/Gas Mark 6 and grease and line a baking tray.

Step 2   Lay the pastry out on a chopping board. Brush the beaten egg all over the top.

Step 3   Sprinkle the cheese over evenly and cut the pastry into approximately 15-16 fingers.

Step 4   Place on the baking tray and bake for 15-20 minutes until crisp, golden, and puffed up.

Recipe 14. Orange and Lemon Cookies

Makes: 12

Preparation Time: 5 minutes

Cooking Time: 30 minutes

The List of Ingredients:

1. ½ teaspoon baking soda.
2. 1 Large Egg

3. 1 cup White Sugar.
4. 1 tbsp Lemon Zest, plus 2 tbsp fresh lemon juice
5. 1/2 cup (1 stick) Butter, softened
6. Pinch of salt
7. 1 tbsp Orange Zest
8. 2 cups All-Purpose Flour

Method:

Step 1 Preheat the oven to 375°F/190°C/Gas Mark 5 and line a large baking tray.

Step 2 Place all of the ingredients into a bowl and beat with a wooden spoon or a hand whisk.

Step 3 When creamed together, place 12 heaps of dough onto the baking tray. Press down a little with the back of a wet fork.

Step 4 Bake for 25-20 minutes until golden and crisp.

Recipe 15. Seed and Herb Muffins

Makes: 12

Prep Time: 5 minutes

Cooking Time: 25 Minutes

The List of Ingredients:

1. 1 tsp Salt
2. 1 tsp Dried Thyme
3. 2 tbsp Parmesan Cheese

4. 1 Egg, beaten
5. 1 tsp Dried Oregano
6. 2 tsp Baking Powder
7. ¾ cup of Milk
8. 2/3 cup of Olive Oil
9. 2 tbsp Melted Butter
10. 2 cups All-Purpose Flour

Method:

Step 1   Preheat an oven to 375°F/190°C/Gas Mark 5 and line a 12-hole muffin tin with cases.

Step 2   Place all of the ingredients into a bowl then mix together. It is important not to overwork a muffin mix so the bake remains soft and fluffy.

Step 3   Divide the mix evenly between the cases and bake for 20 to 25 mins until risen and golden.

Recipe 16. Protein Bakes

Makes: 12

Prep Time: 3 Minutes

Cooking Time: 25-30 Minutes

The List of Ingredients:

1. 1 cup of Oat Flour (blend some rolled oats yourself)
2. 1 Egg, beaten
3. 1 tsp Baking Soda

4. 1 tbsp Protein Powder
5. 4 tbsp Maple Syrup
6. 4 tbsp Chopped Pecan Nuts
7. ¾ cup / 6oz Butter, softened
8. 1 cup of All-Purpose Flour
9. 2 tbsp Flaxseeds
10. 2 tbsp Brown Sugar
11. 2 tbsp Sesame Seeds

Method:

Step 1   Preheat the oven to 375°F/190°C/Gas Mark 5 and line a large baking tray.

Step 2   Cream the butter, maple syrup, and sugar together, until light and fluffy. Add the egg and beat well. Mix in all of the other ingredients and combine.

Step 3   Place heaped teaspoons of this mix onto the baking tray. Bake for 25-30 minutes until golden.

Recipe 17. Cheese and Chive Soda Bread Balls

Makes: 16 Balls

Prep Time: 5 Minutes

Cooking Time: 10-15 Minutes

The List of Ingredients:

1. 1 tsp Seat Salt
2. 3 tbsp Chopped Chives

3. 3 cups of All-Purpose Flour
4. 2 cups of Buttermilk
5. 1 tsp Baking Soda
6. 2/3 cup Grated Cheddar

Method:

Step 1   Preheat the oven to 375°F/190°C/Gas Mark 5 and grease and line a baking tray.

Step 2   Mix all of the ingredients together until just combined. Roll into 16 balls and add to the prepared baking tray.

Step 3   Bake for 10-15 minutes until risen and golden.

Tip: You could make this into 1 large loaf but increase the cooking time.

Recipe 18. Shortbread

Makes: 12

Prep Time: 10 Minutes

Cooking Time: 30 Minutes

The List of Ingredients:

1. ½ cup White Sugar
2. Cold Water to mix
3. 1 tsp Vanilla Extract

4. 1 cup / 7oz Butter, unsalted, and fridge cold
5. 2 cups All-Purpose Flour

Method:

Step 1   Preheat the oven to 350°F/180°C/Gas Mark 4 and line a large baking tray.

Step 2   Cut the butter into small cubes. Add the flour and butter to a bowl and using your fingertips, rub the butter cubes in. Keep going until the flour looks like fine breadcrumbs and there are no lumps.

Step 3   Stir in the sugar and vanilla and enough water to make the mix into a firm dough. Wrap in cling film and place in the fridge for 2 hours.

Step 4   Roll the dough out to 1" thickness. Cut 12 fingers from the dough and lay on the baking tray.

Step 5   Bake for 25-30 minutes, until cooked and just a little colored.

Recipe 19. Blondies

Makes: 9

Prep Time: 15 minutes

Cook Time: 25 minutes

The List of Ingredients:

1. Pinch of Salt
2. 2 tbsp Light Corn Syrup
3. ¾ cup of Light Brown Sugar

4. 2 Eggs, beaten
5. 2/3 cup Butter, softened
6. 1 cup of White Chocolate Chips
7. 1 ½ tsp Vanilla Extract
8. ½ tsp Baking Powder
9. 1 1/3 cups of Flour

Method:

Step 1 Preheat the oven to 375°F/190°C/Gas Mark 5 and line or a square 8"x8" baking tin.

Step 2 Using an electric mixer, beat the sugar and butter together. Add the eggs, syrup, and vanilla and mix again well. Mix in the flour, salt, and baking powder, and then stir in the chocolate chips.

Step 3 Tip the mix into the baking tin and place in the oven for 25-30 minutes until the edges are crisping up, the top is cooked but still a little soft. This should not be overbaked as a blondie should be just baked and still gooey.

Recipe 20. Tomato and Mozzarella Puffs

Makes: 4

Prep Time: 5 Minutes

Cooking Time: 10-15 Minutes

The List of Ingredients:

1. 2 Large Beefsteak Tomatoes, sliced
2. A small handful of washed Basil Leaves

3. 1 cup of sliced Mozzarella

Method:

Step 1   Preheat the oven to 400°F/200°C/Gas Mark 6 and grease and line a baking tray.

Step 2   Layout the 4 squares of puff pastry and half cut through a ½" border around the edge, to look like a frame. Don't go all the way through.

Step 3   Layer the sliced tomatoes, basil leaves, and mozzarella slices over the pastry, making sure to leave the border clear.

Step 4   Place in the oven and bake for 15-20 minutes until the pastry is cooked and risen around the edges and the cheese is oozing.

Recipe 21. Mini Toads in A Hole

Makes: 4 serving

Preparation Time: 5 Minutes

Cooking Time: 35 Minutes

The List of Ingredients:

1. 2 tsp Baking Powder
2. 1 cup of Chopped Cooked Sausages
3. 2 tbsp Olive Oil

4. ½ tsp Salt
5. 1 cup of All-Purpose Flour
6. 2 Eggs
7. 1 ¼ cups of Milk

Method:

Step 1   Preheat the oven to 375°F/190°C/Gas Mark 5 and pour the oil into each base of a 12-hole muffin tin. Divide the chopped sausages between them.

Step 2   Bake the sausages for 10 minutes to get everything really hot.

Step 3   Meanwhile, beat the eggs, milk, salt, flour, and baking powder together until the lumps have gone.

Step 4   Remove the tin from the oven and carefully pour the egg mix on top of all the sausages.

Step 5   Return to the oven for a further 15 minutes, until puffed up and golden. Leave to cool for a while in the tin before trying to remove them.

Recipe 22. Cherry Flapjacks

Makes: 9

Prep Time: 5 Minutes

Cooking Time: 40 Minutes

The List of Ingredients:

1. Pinch of Salt
2. ¼ cup of Light Brown Sugar
3. 2 cups of Rolled Oats

4. ¾ cup / 6oz Unsalted Butter
5. 3 tbsp White Corn Syrup
6. 6 tbsp Glace Cherries

Method:

Step 1   Preheat the oven to 375°F/190°C/Gas Mark 5 and line the 9" square baking tray.

Step 2   Heat the butter, corn syrup, and sugar together in a saucepan. When melted, stir in the oats and cherries.

Step 3   Press into the baking tray and cook for 35-40 minutes, until crisp and golden.

Recipe 23. Pea and Sweetcorn Pancakes

Makes: 8

Preparation Time: 5 minutes

Cooking Time: 10 minutes

The List of Ingredients:

1. 1/3 cup of Sweetcorn kernels
2. 1/3 cup of defrosted peas

3. 2 tsp Baking Powder
4. 1 cup of Milk
5. 1/3 cup of Grated Cheese
6. ½ tsp Salt
7. 2 tbsp Olive Oil to cook
8. 1 tbsp Butter, melted
9. 1 cup of All-Purpose Flour
10. 2 Eggs

Method:

Step 1　Beat the eggs, milk, butter, flour, baking powder, and salt together until the lumps have gone.

Step 2　Stir in the vegetables and cheese.

Step 3　Heat the olive oil in a frying pan. In batches, cook tablespoons of the mix for 3-4 minutes on both sides.

Step 4　Eat immediately or store in the fridge.

Recipe 24. Pizza Wheels

Makes: Approximately 10

Prep Time: 5 Minutes

Cooking Time: 25 Minutes

The List of Ingredients:

1. ½ cup of Chopped Ham
2. 1 cup of Grated Mozzarella
3. 1 Large Sheet of Puff Pastry

4. 1-2 tbsp Milk
5. ¾ cup of Homemade/Jar Tomato Sauce
6. 1 tbsp Dried Oregano

Method:

Step 1   Preheat the oven to 375°F/190°C/Gas Mark 5 and grease and line a baking tray.

Step 2   Lay the pastry onto a chopping board. Spread the tomato sauce all over but leave a margin down one side. Scatter the cheese, herbs, and ham over the base evenly.

Step 3   Roll up the pastry from the side opposite the edge with the margin. Brush with a little milk on the margin to help it "glue" the edge down.

Step 4   Slice into approximately 10 rolls. Turn them on their sides and place on the baking tray.

Step 5   Bake for 25 minutes until puffed up and golden.

Recipe 25. Death by Chocolate Cookies

Makes: 24 Cookies

Prep Time: 15 Minutes

Cook Time: 20-25 Minutes

The List of Ingredients:

1. ¼ tsp Salt
2. 1 cup Dark Chocolate Chips

3. 1 tsp Vanilla Extract
4. ¾ cup Butter, cubed
5. 1/3 cup of Light Brown Sugar
6. ½ cup of Flour
7. 8oz Dark or Milk Chocolate
8. 1 cup of Sugar
9. 2/3 cup Cocoa Powder
10. 3 Eggs, beaten
11. 1 ½ tsp Baking Powder
12. 1 cup White Chocolate Chips

Method:

Step 1   Preheat the oven to 375°F/190°C/Gas Mark 5 and line or grease 2x baking trays.

Step 2   Melt the 8oz of dark or milk chocolate in a glass bowl, over a pan of simmering water. Add the butter and stir until liquid. Cool a little.

Step 3   Tip in the vanilla, sugars, and eggs and beat until a thick dough is formed. Drop tablespoons of the mix onto the baking trays, leaving space to spread.

Step 4   Bake for 20-25 minutes until colored but still soft in the center. Cool on a wire rack and eat within 4-5 days.

Recipe 26. Vanilla and Chocolate Pikelets

Makes: 12

Prep Time: 5 Minutes

Cooking Time: 10 Minutes

The List of Ingredients:

1. 1 tsp Vanilla Extract
2. 2 Large Eggs

3. 2 ½ tsp Baking Powder
4. 1 ½ cups of Milk
5. ¼ cup of Chocolate Chips
6. 1-2 tbsp melted Butter or Olive Oil to Cook
7. 2 cups of All-Purpose Flour
8. ½ tsp Salt
9. 1 tbsp Light Corn Syrup

Method:

Step 1   Beat the eggs, vanilla, and milk together well. Stir in the corn syrup. Gradually add the flour, baking powder, and salt and beat until all the lumps have gone.

Step 2   Stir in the chocolate chips.

Step 3   Heat the oil or butter in a large frying pan. Add tablespoons of the mix to the hot fat and cook. After 3-4 minutes and browned on one side flip over and cook for a further 2-3 minutes. Remove from the heat and continue to cook until all of the batters are used.

Recipe 27. Chocolate Hazelnut Kisses

Makes: 20 Cookies

Prep Time: 20 minutes,

Cook Time: 25 minutes

The List of Ingredients:

1. 1/3 cup of Butter, softened
2. 3/4 cup of Sugar
3. 1 1/3 cups of ground hazelnuts

4. 1 ¾ cups of Flour

Filling:

1. ½ cup of Chocolate Hazelnut Spread
2. 1/3 cup of Heavy Cream

Method:

Step 1   Preheat the oven to 375°F/190°C/Gas Mark 5 and line or grease 2x baking trays.

Step 2   Beat the butter and sugar together until creamy and well combined. Stir in the flour and ground hazelnuts to form a stiff dough.

Step 3   Form into small balls (you want to aim to make about 40) and press them down slightly onto the trays. Bake for 20-25 minutes until golden and cooked. You may need to do this in batches.

Step 4   Cool on a wire rack.

Step 5   Heat the hazelnut spread in a glass bowl in the microwave for 20-30 minutes until quite runny. Stir in the cream and mix until combined. Cool completely.

Step 6   When the filling is cold and thickened and the cookies have cooled, sandwich two together using the filling.

Recipe 28. Chocolate Hazelnut Spread (AKA "Nutella") Brownies

Serves: 9

Prep Time: 15 minutes

Cooking Time: 25 Minutes

The List of Ingredients:

1. 2 Eggs
2. 2/3 cup of All-Purpose Flour

3. 8oz Chocolate Hazelnut Spread

Method:

Step 1   Preheat the oven to 375°F/190°C/Gas Mark 5 and grease and line a 9" square cake tin.

Step 2   Beat the eggs until they are full of air and twice the size. This may take 5-6 minutes depending on your mixer and is definitely one for a powered hand whisk!

Step 3   Heat the chocolate spread in a microwave for 20-30 seconds to soften.

Step 4   Carefully fold in the flour and chocolate spread into the eggs and pour into the prepared tin.

Step 5   Bake for 25 minutes until cooked on the top but still quite squidgy in the middle.

Recipe 29. Coconut & Raspberry Oaties

Makes: 15

Prep Time: 4 Minutes

Cooking Time: 25-30 Minutes

The List of Ingredients:

1. ½ tsp Baking Soda
2. ½ cup of Butter, softened

3. ½ cup of Desiccated Coconut
4. ½ tsp Baking Powder
5. ½ cup of White Sugar
6. 1 cup of All-Purpose Flour
7. 1 cup of Rolled Oats
8. ½ cup of fresh Raspberries
9. ½ cup of Light Brown Sugar

Method:

Step 1   Preheat the oven to 375°F/190°C/Gas Mark 5 and line a large baking tray.

Step 2   Cream the butter and the sugars together until light and fluffy. Add the flour, baking soda, baking powder, oats, and desiccated coconut. Mix well. Add the raspberries and beat in until they are quite broken down and turn the mix to a little pink.

Step 3   Add heaped teaspoons of the dough to the baking tray. Press down a little with a damp hand.

Step 4   Bake for 25-30 minutes until golden and cooked.

Recipe 30. Cornflake and Marshmallow Cakes

Makes: 12

Prep Time: 4 minutes

The List of Ingredients:

1. 3/8 cup / 3oz Butter
2. 4 tbsp Light Corn Syrup
3. 8 cups /7oz Cornflakes
4. 3 tbsp Mini Marshmallows

5. 1 1/3 cups /7oz Dark Chocolate Chips

Method:

Step 1   Melt the chocolate, butter, and corn syrup together in a large saucepan.

Step 2   Stir in the cornflakes and carefully mix until everything is coated well.

Step 3   Fill a 12-hole muffin tin with cupcake cases. Divide the mix between the cases.

Step 4   Scatter over the mini marshmallows. Store in the fridge to set.

Printed in Great Britain
by Amazon